GLAD HE IS OUR DAD

Written by James Tonner and Kelly Tonner

Illustrated by Brad Tonner

ISBN: 1475006055
ISBN-13: 9781475006056

This book is dedicated to Kelly Tonner
fairy tales do come true...

and to our Father
who we were always
Glad to call our Dad

All THE BEST

Jim AND BRAD
TANNER

GLAD HE IS OUR DAD

Written by James Tonner and Kelly Tonner
Illustrated by Brad Tonner

My dad worked in a lily pad factory.

He was in charge of all the toads,
frogs, turtles and tadpoles.

One day they closed the lily
pad factory and dad lost his job.

Dad was very sad when he came home.

At dinner he told us all that until he found another job, he would not be able to do some of the things we did before. Things like traveling, bringing us new toys and going to the amusement park would just have to wait.

Dad felt very bad about this and
he was sorry he had let us down.

We could still play in the pond

and go jumping like we always did.

We could still play leap frog

And we can still sit by the campfire and toast marshmallows.

We could still go on hikes and watch
the sunset at the end of a beautiful day

And
He would still take us for rides

We could still play on the
swings in the park

And
Play games in the backyard

We can sit on the lily pad on a warm
summer night and count the stars

And
We would still end each day
reading a bedtime story.

For such a wonderful dad he can be so silly sometimes.
He should know we do not care about more toys and
traveling or even going to the amusement park.

He should not feel bad.

WE ARE JUST GLAD HE IS OUR DAD

Made in the USA
San Bernardino, CA
14 January 2015